Navigating the Financial Waters

Waters

Lessons from Experienced Investors

Table of Contents

Chapter 1. Introduction

In our Special Report "Navigating the Financial Waters: Lessons from Experienced Investors", we delve into the depths of the investment world, gathering pearls of wisdom from seasoned voyagers of this challenging seascape. This isn't your everyday technical manual filled with jargon. Instead, it's a friendly guide, bursting with insightful stories, practical advice, and actionable lessons from those who have charted successful courses through turbulent financial tides. This special report is designed to inspire, motivate, and equip newcomers and veteran investors alike to captain their own financial ship with confidence. Won't you join us on this exciting journey towards mastering the art of investment? Your financial future awaits!

Chapter 2. Setting Sail: Understanding Investment Basics

In any venture, it's essential to understand the basics and familiarize yourself with the map before setting a course. Similarly, this journey into the investment world begins with comprehending its foundational elements.

2.1. Understanding Investing

Investing can be seen as the practice of committing money or resources to an endeavor with the expectation of attaining additional income or profit. The endeavor can range from purchasing stocks in the stock market to investing in a startup business. At the heart of investing is the concept of risk and return. The risk associated with an investment refers to the level of uncertainty in achieving the returns on the investment. The potential return, on the other hand, is the gain expected from the investment. Usually, higher risk investments often have the potential for higher returns and vice versa.

Investors generate profit from their investments mainly through two avenues: capital gains and income payments. Capital gain is the increase in an investment's price from the time it was bought to the time it's sold. Income payments, on the other hand, are payouts that companies give to their shareholders such as dividends or interests.

2.2. Different Types of Investments

Investments can be broadly categorized into four types: stocks, bonds, mutual funds/ETFs and real estate.

1. Stocks: When you buy shares of a company, you're buying a piece of that company. Stocks, also known as shares or equities, represent ownership in a corporation and grant the shareholder a claim on a portion of the company's assets and earnings.

2. Bonds: A bond is a debt instrument wherein an investor loans money to an entity which borrows the funds for a pre-defined period at a specific interest rate. The company or government issuing the bond uses the loan for various projects or activities, and pay the investor regular interest payments. Upon maturity, the principal amount is returned to the investor.

3. Mutual Funds/Exchange Traded Funds (ETFs): These are investments that pool money from many investors and use it to buy a wide range of different investments, such as stocks and bonds. This allows individual investors to diversify their investments, which can help spread out risk.

4. Real Estate: This involves purchasing physical property. Most investors make money from this type of investment through rental income or by selling the property after its value has increased.

2.3. Deciphering Market Trends

It's crucial to understand market trends as part of the investment basics. Trends give insight into investor sentiment and can be a useful tool for determining when to enter or exit a particular investment. The two main types of trends are uptrends and downtrends. An uptrend implies that prices are generally increasing, and a downtrend indicates that prices are generally falling.

Keeping up-to-date with financial news, understanding economic indicators, and keeping an eye on the general state of the market are recommended practices for any investor aiming to accurately decipher market trends.

2.4. Risk and Return: The Balancing Act

One of the most critical aspects of investing is understanding the relationship between risk and return. The term 'risk' refers to the probability that the actual return on an investment may be different from the expected return. The 'return', conversely, is the money you make from an investment.

There's an indirect relation between risk and return - typically, the higher the return you want to achieve, the higher the risk you have to be willing to accept. Diversification and knowledge, however, can help you moderate the level of risk you face.

2.5. The Power of Compound Interest

The concept of compound interest is a powerful aspect of investing. It is the interest earned on both the initial money invested, known as the principal, and any interest already earned. Albert Einstein famously said, "Compound interest is the eighth wonder of the world. He who understands it, earns it; he who doesn't, pays it." This indicates the crucial role that compound interest plays in building wealth and the detrimental effects it can have when it works against you, such as in the case of debt.

To conclude, understanding the investment basics marks the first step in your investment journey. Essentially, it comes down to buying an asset at a price and hoping the price increases for you to sell at a profit, or it provides an income over time. With a thorough grasp of the basics, you are now ready to delve deeper into the specifics of investment strategies, portfolio management, and advanced concepts such as derivatives and alternative investments. But remember, every successful venture is a result of patience, diligence, and perseverance, and the realm of investment is no exception.

Chapter 3. The Compass: Identifying Your Investment Goals

Just as a sea voyager wouldn't set forth without a destination, an investor shouldn't embark on their financial expedition without clear goals. Financial objectives serve as your investment compass, guiding every decision and strategy therein. Absent an investment goal, you drift adrift, susceptible to the tide of market dangers.

3.1. The Importance of Identifying Your Investment Goals

When it comes to investing, identifying your objectives is half the battle won. Did you know that your aims have a tremendous impact on both your short and long-term investment strategy? Yes, they determine your asset allocation, the kind of financial products you choose, the risk you're willing to take, and the expected returns on your investment. They become the guiding light that leads you through your investment journey.

The first step is understanding what you want to achieve with your investments. Are you aiming for wealth accumulation? Are you investing for retirement? Or perhaps, you're funding your child's education or buying a house. You might even have multiple goals.

By identifying clear investment goals, you don't stray from the path. You stay focused, make deliberate choices about your money allocation and are more likely to succeed in your financial journey.

3.2. The Genesis of Setting Your Investment Goals - Self-awareness

Self-awareness is a crucial requirement in setting your investment goals. It involves understanding your financial circumstances, earnings, expenditures, savings, and your financial commitments. Without an understanding of your current situation, setting realistic goals would be an uphill task.

You need to assess your risk tolerance. Are you a risk-averse investor who gets sleepless nights with market dips? Or are you a risk-taker keen on high-risk, high-reward portfolios? Remember, there's no 'one-size-fits-all' when it comes to risk-taking. What works for others may not work for you. Understanding your risk tolerance is essential to align your investment goals and strategies.

Additionally, understanding your investment horizon is pivotal in setting your goals. Are you in for the long haul? Or are you looking to make quick gains? Short-term investments and long-term investments require different strategies, and your financial objectives should mirror this.

3.3. Crafting Your Investment Goals - The SMART Approach

The acronym 'SMART' perfectly describes an effective way to articulate your investment goals. It stands for; Specific, Measurable, Attainable, Relevant, and Time-bound.

Specific

Your objectives should be well-defined and clear. Avoid vague goals like "I want to make a lot of money". Instead, target something specific like "I want to accumulate $1million for my retirement by investing $500 per month in diverse portfolios".

Measurable

Your target should be quantifiable, enabling you to track your progress. Using the above example, the measurable aspect is accumulating $1 million.

Attainable

Set realistic objectives considering your income and other financial obligations. If your income doesn't allow you to spare $500 monthly for investing, then accumulating $1 million might not be a feasible goal.

Relevant

Your goal should align with your broader financial plans. For instance, if your utmost priority is buying a house, then ensure your investment goals do not divert resources from this priority.

Time-bound

Every goal should have a target date or duration. This creates a sense of urgency and serves as a motivator to stay on track.

Following the SMART approach, here's an example of an investment goal: "Invest $500 per month in a diverse portfolio to accumulate $1 million by retirement at 65".

3.4. Rethinking and Refining Your Goals

Investment isn't a set-it-and-forget-it endeavor. Economic crises, financial market fluctuations, and personal circumstances – everything impacts your investments. It's pivotal to revisit your investment objectives periodically and tweak them as necessary.

Annual reviews of your goals and how your investments are faring are the least you should do. In case of substantial changes (good or bad) in your personal or financial circumstances, immediate reassessment is in order.

The journey of an investor is a life-long marathon – not a sprint. Patience, persistence, and adaptability are key to achieving your investment goals. Remember to celebrate the small victories along the passage. After all, each little win brings you one step closer to your ultimate financial destination.

In conclusion, defining and identifying your investment goals is paramount to successful investing. These goals are your compass, guiding your investment decisions and strategies. Reflect on your financial standing, evaluate your risk tolerance, consider your investment horizon, set SMART goals, and ensure to review those goals periodically. With these steps, you're not just a wanderer but a captain steering your financial ship towards your desired destination. Here's to your mastery of the investment art!

Chapter 4. Plotting the Course: Developing an Investment Strategy

Every successful investment journey begins with a plan. No renowned explorer has set out to conquer new lands without a map, and no experienced mariner has embarked on a high seas adventure without charting a path. The same rules apply in the world of investment. Without a well-devised strategy, you risk sailing into the turbulent waters ill-prepared. Here, we discuss the key elements of crafting your investment strategy.

4.1. Understanding Your Financial Landscape:

Before you begin plotting your investment journey, it's crucial to comprehend your financial landscape fully. Understanding your financial state involves a comprehensive review of your income, expenditure, assets, and liabilities. Consider this as an audit to identify your financial strengths, weaknesses, opportunities, and threats.

Your income is the primary source of capital for your investments. It can be either active (salary or business profit) or passive (rental income, dividends, interest). The comparison of your income and expenses gives you a clear picture of how much you can potentially allocate for investment.

Assets and liabilities provide a view into your current net worth. Assets can include property such as a house or car, savings, retirement funds, stocks, bonds, or any other form of investments. Liabilities comprise all your obligations like home mortgage, student loan, credit card debt, medical debt, etc. The difference between your total assets and liabilities equals your net worth.

4.2. Setting Your Investment Goals:

The next crucial step in developing your investment strategy consists of defining and articulating your investment goals. Crystal clear objectives will guide your investment decisions and keep you focused, especially when the financial waters get choppy.

Start by identifying what you want to achieve. Are you investing for retirement, a down payment on a house, your children's college education, or starting your own business? Once you've precisely defined your objectives, break them down into short-term (less than five years), middle-term (five to ten years), and long-term (more than ten years) goals.

After identifying goals, set a monetary value to each goal. Be realistic, consider inflation, and remember that your investment capacity may increase over time with salary hikes or other income avenues.

4.3. Determining Your Risk Tolerance:

Every investment comes with a degree of risk, and understanding your personal risk tolerance is a vital aspect of your investment strategy. Your risk tolerance depends on your financial ability (how much loss you can bear without affecting your lifestyle), your emotional aptitude (how comfortable you are with the idea of losing some or all your investments), and the time frame of your investment.

A high-risk tolerance typically implies that you are comfortable with more volatile investments such as stocks, while low-risk tolerance may steer you towards safer investments like bonds or money market accounts.

Being honest about your risk tolerance is a cornerstone of creating an investment strategy that you can abide by without losing sleep over the state of the market.

4.4. Asset Allocation and Diversification:

Asset allocation means dividing your investments across different asset classes, like stocks, bonds, real estate, to suit your risk tolerance, investment horizon and financial goals. For instance, if you're investing for a long-term goal and comfortable with higher risks, your portfolio might include a higher percentage of equities.

Diversification, or not putting all your eggs in one basket, is a safety measure to maximize returns and minimize risk. It involves spreading investments across a variety of assets within a single asset class or across asset classes. By doing this, you create a buffer as different investments usually don't perform poorly at the same time.

4.5. Regular Reviews and Adjustments:

Finally, your investment journey doesn't end with crafting the right strategy. The investment world is dynamic and unpredictable, and even the best plans require regular review. Market conditions, financial goals, risk tolerance, or personal finances are subjected to change, and your strategy should adapt to these changes.

Scheduling regular reviews of your investment strategy will allow you to make necessary adjustments and stay on course. The frequency of these reviews can be bi-annual or annual, or whenever a significant financial change happens in your life.

This thorough approach to developing your investment strategy would be your compass, guiding you through your financial journey. It will arm you with the right tools to navigate through the choppy waters of the investment world and steer your ship towards your financial objectives. A careful, strategic plan, matched with patience and discipline, will take you from an investment novice to a seasoned investor, one step at a time. Regardless of the setbacks and volatilities you might face, your solid strategy will always shine a light on the path towards your financial goals.

Chapter 5. Choosing Your Vessel: Types of Investment Vehicles

Just as sailors who venture out onto the open ocean need to understand their ship inside and out, so too must investors be intimately familiar with the different types of investment vehicles available. In this journey towards financial independence and success, choosing the right vessel for your goals, risk tolerance, and time horizon is key. Here, we'll delve into a variety of investment vehicles, exploring their pros, cons, and ideal uses.

5.1. Cash Equivalents

Cash is the simplest investment vehicle, effectively serving as your 'lifeboat.' It's accessible, carries low risk, and offers reliable, albeit modest, returns. Cash equivalents include savings accounts, certificates of deposit (CDs), Treasury bills, and money market funds.

Characteristics[Pros]Cons Cash Equivalents^Easy to access and low risk^Lower potential returns

Remember, though stable and reliable, cash equivalents offer returns that often fail to keep pace with inflation. They're well-suited to short-term financial goals or as a portion of a larger, diversified portfolio to provide stability and liquidity.

5.2. Bonds

Speaking of stability, let's shift our gaze towards bonds. A bond is essentially a loan to a government or company, who promises to repay the loan on a specific date, along with regular interest payments.

Characteristics[Pros]Cons Bonds^Regular interest payments, less capital fluctuation^Lower returns compared to equities, subject to interest rate risk

Bonds are typically less volatile than stocks, making them a good counterpart in a diversified portfolio. Nevertheless, they're subject to interest rate risk– as rates rise, bond prices drop. They can be suitable for intermediate to longer-term objectives, depending on the bond's maturity date.

5.3. Stocks

Stocks, or equities, represent a fraction of ownership in a company, offering the potential for higher returns.

Characteristics[Pros]Cons Stocks^High growth potential, Profit share through dividends^Volatile, potential for a complete loss

Investing in stocks offers the potential for robust growth but also comes with added risk, including the possibility of losing your entire investment. Stocks are best suited for long-term financial goals, given that they can withstand market volatility over time.

5.4. Mutual Funds

A mutual fund is an investment vessel that pools money from multiple investors to invest in a diversified portfolio of stocks, bonds, and/or other assets. Managed by professional portfolio managers, these funds give individuals access to diversified investments with a single transaction.

Characteristics[Pros]Cons Mutual Funds^Diversification, professionally managed^Expenses, less control

Mutual funds are a way to obtain diversification, which can help reduce risk, without having to have a large amount of capital. The flip side is that there are expenses associated with these funds, including management fees, that can eat into your returns. Investors also give up some control since the fund manager makes all of the investment decisions.

5.5. Exchange-Traded Funds (ETFs)

ETFs are similar to mutual funds but trade on an exchange like a stock. This structure provides the diversification of a mutual fund with the flexibility of a stock.

Characteristics[Pros]Cons ETFs^Diversification, flexibility in trading, lower fees^Market price may differ from net asset value

Like mutual funds, ETFs offer diversification and are suitable for most financial objectives, depending on the underlying assets. Unlike mutual funds, ETFs can be bought or sold throughout the trading day and often have lower expenses.

5.6. Real Estate

Direct real estate investing involves buying properties to generate income and/or capital appreciation. Just as we wouldn't set sail in a rowboat expecting to traverse the ocean, we wouldn't invest in just any property expecting to realize profitable returns.

Characteristics[Pros]Cons Real Estate^Potential for high returns, physical asset, tax benefits^High upfront costs, liquidity issues, management intensive

Real estate can offer higher returns and cash flow, and it's a tangible asset you can use. However, it's also capital intensive, not very liquid, and can be management-involved, particularly for rental properties.

5.7. Retirement Accounts

Retirement accounts are not so much an 'investment vessel' as a 'navigation tool' that leads to different investment vehicles. These tax-advantaged accounts, including IRAs, 401(k)s, and Defined Benefit Plans, can help you save for retirement more efficiently.

Characteristics[Pros]Cons   Retirement   Accounts^Tax   advantages, potential employer contributions^Limited access to funds before retirement age, contribution limits

Retirement accounts offer significant tax benefits but typically penalize you for accessing funds before retirement age. Your choice in retirement account will depend on your income, employment status, and retirement goals.

As you can see, the world of investing is vast and varied, alike an ocean teaming with potential. The investment vehicles you choose for your financial journey will depend on factors including personal financial goals, risk tolerance, time horizon, and liquidity needs. Remember, diversification is key to managing risk and enhancing potential returns. Happy sailing!

Chapter 6. Benefit of Experience: Lessons from Successful Investors

In the realm of investing, experience truly stands as a torchlight that dispels the shadows of uncertainty. Learning from those who have already navigated the turbulent waters of investment markets can save us from costly pitfalls, while also helping us spot the opportunities that might otherwise be overlooked. In this section, we will be sharing priceless insights garnered from successful investors that underline the various advantages of experience.

6.1. The Power of Patience

One of the most common lessons learned by veteran investors is the power of patience. Warren Buffett, one of the world's most successful investors, once famously said, "The stock market is a device for transferring money from the impatient to the patient." Investing isn't about making quick financial gains; instead, it's about making thoughtful decisions and allowing investments to mature over time.

Several experienced investors echo a similar sentiment. They emphasize not getting swayed by short-term market noises and holding one's ground even during rough financial weather. Historical market trends suggest that those who remain invested in their chosen avenues despite volatility enjoy substantial returns in the long run.

6.2. The Importance of Diversification

Diversification is another essential principle emphasized by successful investors. Holding a variety of asset types can reduce the potential for loss in any single investment. As Ray Dalio, the founder of Bridgewater Associates, asserts, "Diversification is a powerful tool to reduce risk without compromising returns."

In essence, diversification is about not putting all your eggs in one basket. Investors should consider a mix of different asset classes, like stocks, bonds, commodities, and real estate, to spread risk. Furthermore, diversification within an asset category—like different sectors or companies within stocks—is equally important.

6.3. Emotional Stability in Investing

Investing is a test of nerve as much as it is a fiscal challenge. Market volatility can provoke strong emotions that lead to impulsive decisions, often detrimental to one's portfolio. As the legendary investor Benjamin Graham advised, "The investor's chief problem — and even his worst enemy — is likely to be himself."

Graham underscores the importance of not letting emotions dictate your investing decisions. Emotions like fear, greed, or over-excitement can cloud rational thinking. Experienced investors advocate for a balanced, analytical approach, guided by data and not by feelings.

6.4. Value Investing

Value investing, a strategy that involves buying securities that appear underpriced by some form of fundamental analysis, forms the ideological foundation of investing for many successful investors.

Warren Buffet, a student of Benjamin Graham, has always espoused the merits of value investing. He has often narrated stories about his early days, where he learned to buy stocks that were fundamentally strong and undervalued by the market.

Of course, value investing requires careful reading of balance sheets, understanding of the business environment, and patience to wait for the market to recognize the value you've perceived. It means going against the current market sentiment, which is never easy but often rewarding.

6.5. Risk Management

Investment gurus underscore the importance of managing risks efficaciously. Seth Klarman, the billionaire portfolio manager and CEO of the Baupost Group, emphasizes, "Investing is the intersection of economics and psychology. The most important rule is to play great defense, not great offense."

Experienced investors prioritize preserving their capital over chasing high returns. They understand the huge detrimental impact of a significant loss to a portfolio. Therefore, strategic risk management involving stop losses, rebalancing portfolios and hedging plays a key role in their investing philosophy.

6.6. Continual Learning and Adaptability

The investing landscape is constantly evolving. Technologies emerge, economic paradigms shift, new industries rise, while others falter. For this reason, successful investors value continual learning and adaptability.

Ric Edelman, founder of Edelman Financial Engines, asserts, "The key to financial success is not just about making money. It is about staying educated and up-to-date, continually improving your skills and knowledge."

6.7. Conclusion

The insights shared by successful investors are distilled wisdom from years of making, breaking, and remaking their investment strategies. Embracing patience, understanding the power of diversification, maintaining emotional stability, pursuing value, effectively managing risk, and continually learning—these are the broad lessons that successful investors teach us. Incorporating these principles into your investment practice could steer your financial ship safely and successfully through the stormy seas of the investment world.

Chapter 7. Shoals Ahead: Common Investment Pitfalls to Avoid

Approaching the edge of a financial precipice is easier than one might think. The lure of quick profits, the prospect of securing a comfortable future, or just the sheer excitement of engaging with the market can blind even the most watchful navigator to looming perils. Unknown to most, they ply through the dangerous waters encrusted with invisible shoals. It's vital, therefore, to identify and understand these common investment pitfalls in a bid to steer clear of them in your investment journey.

7.1. Understanding The Market Misconceptions

One of the most common mistakes investors make is not understanding the market properly. The stock market isn't a monolithic entity that moves in predictable patterns. Instead, it's a complex ecosystem where various factors such as economic indicators, company performance, and investor sentiment interact in intricate ways. Being aware of these dynamic interactions can save you from financial losses. Remember, knowledge is the most valuable commodity in the world of investing.

7.2. The Lure of Short-Term Trading

Short-term or day trading can be an attractive prospect. After all, who wouldn't want to earn a quick buck overnight? However, the reality of day trading is far more complex and fraught with risks. High brokerage fees, substantial capital requirement and stress are some downsides that can erode not just your profits but your peace of mind as well. In fact, studies have shown that most day traders fail to make consistent profits over the long term. Instead of chasing quick profits, focus on building a diversified, long-term portfolio that aligns with your financial goals.

7.3. Overconfidence and Emotional Decisions

Emotion is a terrible advisor when it comes to investment decisions. Overconfidence can lead to taking on more risk than one can handle, and panic can prod one into selling their stocks during a market correction. Try introducing a level of objectivity into your investment strategy. Create a set of rules or criteria that a potential investment must meet before you put in your money. And once you've made an investment, stick to a predetermined exit strategy.

7.4. Putting All Eggs in One Basket

This old adage holds particularly true in the investment world. Concentrating all your capital in a single stock or asset class can multiply your earnings. However, it also exposes you to potentially devastating losses when things go south. Diversification, or spreading your investments across various asset classes, geographies, and industries, can help mitigate this risk. An effectively diversified portfolio can provide you a steady stream of returns while buffering you against severe market downturns.

7.5. Ignoring Your Risk Tolerance

Every investor has a unique risk tolerance based on their financial situation, investment goals, and personal disposition. Some might be comfortable with significant market volatility, while others may prefer a more conservative approach. Ignoring your risk tolerance can lead to regrettable investment decisions. Understanding and respecting your risk tolerance can help you stay comfortable with your investment strategy, even during a market downturn, and avoid any hasty, emotionally-driven investment decisions.

7.6. Neglecting the Impact of Fees & Taxes

Transaction fees, account maintenance charges, and taxes can eat into your investment returns if not given adequate consideration. Always account for them when evaluating the potential profit of an investment. Some investment modes may seem profitable on the surface, but when the charges are factored in, they might not be as lucrative as you thought. Also, using tax-advantaged accounts can help enhance your after-tax returns.

7.7. Failing to Regularly Review Your Portfolio

A common mistake that investors make is to take a 'set it and forget it' approach towards their portfolio. Regular reviews are essential to ensure that your portfolio aligns with your evolving financial goals and changes in market dynamics. Portfolio rebalancing, or the practice of periodically buying or selling assets to maintain their original asset allocation, could also be an effective strategy to potentially enhance returns and manage risk.

Each of these pitfalls, while common, can be avoided with careful planning, proper understanding, and disciplined execution of investment strategies. Remember, the art of investing isn't about making quick decisions for short-term benefits; rather, it's about making calculated decisions that can potentially offer steady returns over the long-term. Whether you're a beginner or an experienced investor, steering clear of these common shoals can equip you with a robust ship, a starlit course, and the nerve to navigate through the often treacherous, yet rewarding, financial seas.

Chapter 8. The Art of Navigation: Managing Market Volatility

Market turbulence is a constant factor in the world of finance, just as unexpected rough seas can be for an experienced sailor at the helm. Navigating through such volatility and successfully reaching your financial goals requires a blend of strategic planning, keen intuition, and in-depth market knowledge.

===Understanding Market Volatility

Volatility is the rate at which the price of an asset or market increases or decreases for a set of returns. It is most commonly measured by the standard deviation or variance between returns. High volatility means the price of the asset can change dramatically over a short time, making it possible for significant price jumps. On the other hand, low volatility implies that the price does not fluctuate dramatically, but changes at a steady pace over a longer period.

There are two primary types of market volatility: Historical and Implied. Historical volatility refers to the actual past movement of a security, measured from the change in security price over time. Implied volatility, meanwhile, is derived from an option's price and shows market expectations about future volatility. It is essential to understand and monitor both as they provide different insights into the market.

===The Importance of Developing Risk Tolerance

Risk tolerance refers to the degree of variability in investment returns that an investor is willing to stand. Understanding your risk tolerance is a key factor when making investment decisions. Having a grasp on your risk profile will help you determine what types of investments you're comfortable with, how much volatility you can stomach, and what your investing endpoint should look like.

A few factors to consider when determining risk tolerance include financial risk, income risk, capital risk, and personal risk. Financial risk is the possibility of outliving your savings. Income risk involves the potential decrease or loss of income. The risk of capital refers to the decrease in value of an item or investment. Personal risk is where emotional aspects come into play, such as how much stress or worry market fluctuations cause you.

8.1. The Impact of Market Conditions on Investment Performance

Just like the weather can impact sea currents and winds, market conditions dramatically affect the performance of investments. A bullish market, characterized by increasing prices and investor confidence, will offer different opportunities than a bearish market, which denotes falling prices and waning investor confidence. Additionally, external factors such as political stability, market regulations, and international trade agreements can dramatically change the market environment and, consequently, your investment performance.

8.2. Strategies to Navigate Through Volatility

Developing effective strategies can significantly smooth investment journeys through volatile markets. Start by diversifying your investment portfolio. This strategy involves spreading your investments across various assets, classes, sectors, or countries to reduce risk. Remember, volatility in some markets can offset stability in others.

Next, consider a long-term perspective. While market volatility causes prices to fluctuate in the short-term, they tend to average out over longer periods. Long-term investors who stay the course are more likely to see substantial returns on their investments than those who give in to the temptation of constant buying and selling.

8.3. Leveraging Technology for Your Investments

Financial technology tools (FinTech) offer valuable support when navigating volatile markets. These tools provide data-driven insights and can process more information than a human, providing comprehensive market analyses. Tools such as robo-advisors can even automate the investment process, ensuring you stick to your investment strategy and avoid panic-induced or emotion-driven decisions.

8.4. Conclusion

Naturally, sailing through the turbulent seas of market volatility won't always be smooth, but with a deeper understanding of market volatility, an honest appraisal of your risk tolerance, astute awareness of market conditions, a carefully crafted strategy, and a proficient use of technology, you can confidently chart your course through any financial storm. Remember, mastering these skills won't come overnight. But patience, determination, and the pursuit of continuous learning and adaptation will eventually steer your financial ship towards your desired destination, proving to be your life-long ally.

Chapter 9. Sailing in Storms: Strategies for Financial Uncertainties

Should you find yourself adrift in the stormy seas of financial uncertainty, it's essential to have an arsenal of strategies to navigate through. Much like the experienced sea captain: calm, decisive, and equipped with an accurate map and compass, so too, the shrewd investor must finetune his approach to manage potential risks and capitalize on promising opportunities.

9.1. Understanding Uncertainty

Financial uncertainty can be likened to a tempest at sea: sudden, unpredictable, and alarming. However, defining and understanding these uncertainties can significantly alter how you perceive and confront them. Financial uncertainties are basically market fluctuations: they can be due to economic changes, worldwide geopolitical events, or internal organizational issues.

Anticipating uncertainty isn't about predicting specific disasters but being prepared that something – anything – might stir the waters. Like a wise captain plots alternative courses to account for possible storms, being informed and versatile are vital components in an investor's navigation toolkit.

9.2. Identifying Risks

Just as meteorologists identify potential storms on the horizon, as an investor, you need to identify and assess the potential risks on your financial journey. A prudent method is risk analysis, which can reveal how sensitive your portfolio may be to various uncertainties.

First, gather as much information as possible about your investments and the circumstances surrounding them. Educating yourself about market trends, economic indicators, and corporate performances is an essential first step, as knowledge will be the backbone of your risk identification process.

Next, evaluate the impact these uncertainties can have on your portfolio. This step may involve constructing scenarios that show possible outcomes. Much like a sailor understanding how different storm strengths could impact their journey, you need to understand which events will rock your financial vessel, and by how much.

9.3. Creating a Robust Portfolio

To stay afloat in financially uncertain times, your investment portfolio needs to be as sturdy and balanced as a well-constructed ship. Diversifying your investment across a variety of sectors and asset classes can provide a buffer against market volatility, much like a ship's balance helps it stay upright during a storm.

It's important to understand that balance in your investment does not mean dividing your wealth equally across different asset types. Just as a ship has more weight in its bottom to keep it steady, you may sometimes need to go heavy in a certain asset type or sector based on market conditions and your financial goals.

However, diversification should also happen within asset classes. It's not enough just to invest in "stocks" or "bonds": these categories house a broad selection of companies and governments with diverse prospects and risks.

9.4. Building in Flexibility

In sailing terms, 'tacking' is a maneuver whereby a sailing vessel, whose desired course is into the wind, changes its direction repeatedly to make headway. Just as a good sailor is prepared to change course and tack against the wind, as an investor, you must be prepared for quick shifts in strategy.

Your investment plan shouldn't be an unbreakable contract but rather an adaptive guide designed to be flexible in times of financial turbulence. The investment climate is perpetually evolving due to technological advancements, regulatory changes, and shifts in investor attitudes. Therefore, an investor's ability to adapt predictably volatile stock market conditions is an invaluable skill.

Staying liquid, or having a safe and accessible cash reserve, creates room for this flexibility. With a sound liquidity plan, you can seize promising investment opportunities or cushion the impact of a sudden financial storm.

9.5. Weathering the Storm

Sometimes, despite all precautions, the storm hits hard. These times call for strategy, patience, and a certain level of stoicism. Panicking and hastily changing your investment course can often lead to regrettable decisions.

Remember, bad weather at sea doesn't last forever, and neither do financial storms. Stay committed to your long-term strategies and maintain perspective during these choppy periods. And, remember the wisdom of seasoned investors who remind us that volatility is not always a sign of long-term loss. Indeed, for those who understand its nature, volatility can even create exploitable opportunities.

Navigating through financial uncertainties may seem daunting, but with well-planned strategies, risk identification, portfolio diversification, flexibility and resilience, it's a sea that can be not only be crossed, but conquered. Probable storms should never deter a well-equipped investor from their journey, because, as every seasoned mariner knows, the roughest seas often make the best sailors. Indeed, the same could be said for investors.

Chapter 10. Uncharted Waters: Exploring New Investment Opportunities

The vast and open ocean of investing can seem daunting to even the seasoned sailor. Herein lay uncharted waters, teeming with chances to discover new lands of opportunity, yet also fraught with unknown dangers. Learning to navigate these waters, while challenging, is critical for achieving financial prosperity.

10.1. Setting Sail: Identifying New Investment Opportunities

First, unbolt the compass of curiosity. Consider reading periodicals, industry reports, and listening to podcasts, to keep abreast with current trends. Renewable energy, technology, biotech, and the gig economy are some prime areas where potential new opportunities could be lurking.

Once an opportunity has been spotted in these periscopes, it must be evaluated. Is it a passing ship, or a true island of opportunity? This requires a rigorous process of due diligence.

10.2. The Map: Conducting Due Diligence

Due diligence involves thoroughly researching and understanding the investment. It is the lighthouse that can guide investors safely to the shore.

Here, financial statements become your leading stars. Income statements, balance sheets, and cash flow statements can reveal imperative insights about a company's health. Look at revenue trends, expense ratios, debt levels, and how much cash the company generates.

Also, it's crucial to understand the company's business model. How does it make money? What is its competitive advantage? Who is its competition and how is it performing against them?

10.3. Charting the Course: Risk Analysis

In this rough sea of investing, not all waters are equally navigable. An understanding of risks associated with each investment proposition is fundamental.

The pivotal question here is 'How much can I potentially lose?'. VaR (Value at Risk) is a statistical technique to assess this risk. However, while VaR provides a measure, it doesn't insulate against losses.

10.4. Current and Tides: The Market Trends

Navigating the marketplace requires a keen sense of direction. It is about understanding how the market is moving and foreseeing how these trends might shape the future.

Look at the economic factors. Are interest rates rising or falling? How is the job market? Major nautical indicators are GDP growth rates, unemployment rates, and inflation.

Next, consider the industry trends. Is there rapid growth or is the industry facing extinction like the dinosours? Look at the key sector leaders. How are they doing?

10.5. The Voyage: Crafting an Investment Strategy

Our ship is now ready to set sail. It's time to craft the investment strategy that will guide the voyage.

A strategy must detail when to buy, what to buy, and when to sell. It needs balance and diversification. Herein is the importance of the portfolio theory, which advocates holding a well-diversified portfolio to spread risk.

Set clear objectives and stick to them. Are you seeking growth, income, or both? Your answer will significantly influence the choice of investment.

10.6. Land in Sight: Making the Investment Decision

Making the decision to invest is like finally sighting land. It requires courage and decisiveness. However, remember that the decision doesn't end at buying. Regular monitoring of the investment is critical to ensure it is meeting the desired objectives.

These uncharted waters could seem intimidating, but with the right navigation aids and a sense of adventure, the voyage could become a rewarding journey towards wealth creation. Ready to set sail?

In the next chapter, we'll navigate through 'Troubled Waters: Managing Investment Risks'. Keep your compass handy!

Chapter 11. Safe Harbor: Planning your Financial Retirement

Just as any competent mariner would not risk setting out on the high sea without specifics of the journey and a well-crafted plan, the voyage into your financial retirement requires precise navigation and extensive consideration. It necessitates a holistic understanding of a diverse range of disciplines, such as understanding your income, debt, investments, and future goals.

11.1. Navigating your Retirement Income

Understanding your retirement income sources is the first step in planning your financial retirement. Every imaginable source of income in retirement must be accounted for. This could include pensions, your retirement savings, Social Security benefits, income from real estate rental, part-time employment income, or even an inheritance.

One glaring challenge for many is Social Security. It is a lifeline, yet it's commonly misunderstood. Obtaining clarity on the amount you're likely to receive from Social Security helps determine the gap you need to fill with your retirement savings. The Social Security benefits estimate can be found on the Social Security Administration's website. Download your statement, familiarize yourself with it, and integrate it into your retirement income plan.

11.2. Understanding Debt in Retirement

Eliminating debt before retirement can lead to significant financial relief since servicing debt can consume a substantial chunk of your retirement income. From mortgages to credit card debt, loans, and other obligations, unmanaged debt can sink your retirement plan faster than you think.

Before paying off your debts, it's important to understand the terms and conditions attached to each of them. Pay particular attention to interest rates - those debts with particularly high interest rates might need to be prioritized.

Part of your pre-retirement plan could also include reducing your living expenses. This can be achieved by downsizing. Selling your home to move into a smaller, cheaper one could provide you additional funds to manage your debts and even add to your retirement savings.

11.3. The Engine of Growth: Smart Investments

Your investments are the engine of your retirement financial plan. They provide you with the financial security that savings alone cannot offer. Creating a balanced and well-diversified portfolio, with a mix of assets, can help mitigate risks while aiming for better returns.

Your investments should be guided by principles such as your risk tolerance, expected returns, and time horizons. If you're unsure about any aspect of your investment strategy, it could be beneficial to seek advice from a financial advisor. They can provide guidance on allocating your funds wisely and selecting investments that suit your long-term goals.

Bonds, stocks, real estate, mutual funds, and exchange-traded funds (ETFs) are diverse options each with varying degrees of risk and returns. Annuities and life insurance can also be worthy considerations given their potential to secure a steady stream of income during retirement.

11.4. Safeguarding your Financial Health

Retirement does not exempt you from unanticipated expenses. Health care costs, family emergencies, major home repairs, and other unexpected costs can eat into your income. Having an emergency fund of three to six months' worth of living expenses offers a safety net to protect your retirement savings.

It's also essential to be proactive about monitoring and protecting your credit. Fraud and identity theft can be crippling. Check your credit reports regularly, set up fraud alerts, and consider investing in identity theft protection services.

11.5. Estate Planning: Ensuring your Assets are Protected

Estate planning is not only for the immensely wealthy. Everyone can benefit from having a plan in place that dictates what happens to their assets once they pass away or become incapacitated. A will, a power of attorney, and a living trust are a few tools that can be used. Furthermore, considering tax implications and coordinating your retirement plan with your estate plan can save your estate substantial amounts in taxes and fees.

11.6. Building a Resilient Retirement Plan

Building a resilient retirement plan, capable of withstanding market downturns and unforeseen life events, should be your ultimate objective. This plan should provide not only a reliable income stream but also ensure sustainability in line with your projected lifespan. It should incorporate various sources of income, realistic spending patterns, and inflation. Performing regular checkups and adjusting your plan as needed is vital to ensuring its longevity and relevance.

Your financial retirement isn't something to be left to chance. It requires careful planning, understanding, and regular readjusting. This is your journey. Let these guidelines direct you towards a safe harbor, where you'll find the serenity and financial security you worked so hard to earn.